Billionaires Prefer Single Moms

A Single Mom's Guide to Purpose, Prosperity, and Partnership

Maisha S. Akbar, Ph.D.

Author: Maisha S. Akbar
www.billionairesperfersinglemoms.com

Published by: Blackplaybook Productions, Inc.
www.blackplaybook.com

Editor: Samatha McCroy

Cover Design: Jazmine Newsome

Table of Contents

Acknowledgements

All praise is due to God!

Oh Lord, make me and my children steadfast in prayer. Oh Lord, accept the prayer. Our Lord forgive me and my parents and the believers on the day of judgement. Amen.

By God's grace I received highly valued emotional and technical support on this project. I am truly thankful.

Introduction

#singlemomsmatter

#singlemommagic

#singlemommiracles

I never knew exhaustion like this before! Raising two toddlers as a new single mom kicked my butt daily! My youngest, who was teething, could talk in full sentences, yet could not use the potty. And did I mention she was also nursing? My oldest, the epitome of a rambunctious, rumbling, tumbling, testosterone driven, three-year-old boy, demanded a lot of physical and mental stimulation. During the day, they always seemed to be running in opposite directions. After dark, my baby girl would not, could not sleep through the night, and she wouldn't until kindergarten. Having recently relocated to a new town to create a new life, I had no regrets about my decision to leave their father after a volatile, four-plus year relationship. However, when I left him, I also left the limited help (no tea, no shade) he provided in keeping them safe and sound. I now faced doing a job meant for (at least) two all alone.

I had no crystal ball to see what my new life as a single mom would look like. I had no manual to help me foresee the challenges, manage my resources, and plan for our futures. I was 100% committed to my responsibilities, but I longed for a "big picture" of what I needed to keep in mind as I proceeded.

On top of everything else, I'd recently entered a Ph.D. program at the University of Texas at Austin. Needless to say, the coursework and degree requirements were demanding. I pursued an advanced degree in a field, Communications Studies, about which I was passionate, ensuring I would always do work I loved. I did so despite being repeatedly asked by naysayers, "what are you going to do with a degree in that field," which reflected others' lack of understanding of my career path. Undaunted, I followed my life's calling, making my journey more like a quest instead of a burden. As such, I entered into this new phase of my life with curiosity and a sense of adventure, not fear or dread. It was a long, hard road, but in the words of Maya Angelou, a prolific artist, author, and fellow single mom, "I wouldn't take nothing for my journey now."

Now, more than twenty years later, I am a veteran single mom who has raised her children alone, earned a Ph.D. and tenure, as well as attracted a love of my life. Through *Billionaires Prefer Single Moms* (BPSM), I am happy (ecstatic even) to share my story in the hopes of inspiring single moms like me who would appreciate having a road map to guide them along their paths. I am here to share my experiences, the highs, as well as the lows, helping single moms navigate their journeys, which, by all accounts, overwhelms the best of us. Not only that, I want to help single moms do so with a sense of wholeness, high self-worth, and abundance. I want to help single moms fully realize their experiences as spiritual exercises from which the best life has to offer proceeds.

Billionaires Prefer Single Moms (BPSM) offers single moms a guide to love, wealth, and happiness. Both aspirational and inspirational, BPSM's title plays off that of a 1953 feature film titled, *Gentlemen Prefer Blondes*, starring Hollywood bombshell Marilyn Monroe. Even further, an online article published in 2014 titled, "Billionaires Prefer Black Wives," first reimagined Black women as ultimately desirable to the world's richest men. Finally, *Billionaires Prefer Single Moms* characterizes my own love journey, which culminated in attracting my "Billionaire Boo" whose goals reflect an abundant mindset mirroring my high(er) self-worth.

My story is largely made up of a transformational journey to loving myself, holding myself to a higher standard, and attracting a true love, a Billionaire Boo. My journey is a primarily spiritual one, especially important since, as a single mom, I can consult very few visual references. Not only are images of single moms left out of larger cultural narratives, but, when finally encountered, the "single mom story" is generally met with suspicion, ignored, misinterpreted, or otherwise invalidated. In short, I've been hard pressed to find stories reflecting my values, aspirations, and true worth as a single mom. Finding images representing single moms like me as valuable contributors to society is like looking for a needle in a haystack!

Single moms lead extremely busy lives, juggling the care of our children, managing households, as well as working and/or going to school. Consequently, our spiritual, physical, and emotional needs often get put on the back burner, which makes our experience even more frustrating! We don't make time to examine our thoughts, feelings, and actions about love, money, and career goals. Even worse, we are often isolated and subject to societal stigmas and standards that further keep us away from the information and support we need.

Billionaires Prefer Single Moms provides affirmation and perspective, as well as a program for any single mom whose busy life distracts her from attracting a life that is worthy of her. It is my hope that BPSM cuts the time it takes for single moms to improve their dating lives, financial stability, and public (or societal) images. A single mom who uses the strategies outlined in *Billionaires Prefer Single Moms* can significantly reduce her learning curve, as well as her growing pains. *Billionaires Prefer Single Moms* provides a plan that single moms can immediately use to implement self-determined change.

Praise God! As a result of listening to my heart early in my journey and staying true to myself in the face of overwhelming discouragement, I found a way to love myself and pursue my dreams. *Billionaires Prefer Single Moms* supports all single moms in their journeys to self-love, as well as romantic love.

I invite you to visit www.BillionairesPreferSingleMoms.com for additional free resources and training.

Chapter One

Questions for Thought

Did you buy into society's definition of love and marriage only to, after having kids, end up disillusioned and disappointed?

Did you (marry and) have children before you figured out your true worth?

Were you sexually, emotionally, or physically abused as a child and bore your own children before you'd fully matured?

Have you raised your children alone?

Have you long sacrificed your love life to achieve career goals or family stability?

Have you not loved again after a divorce, death, or separation even though it's been a long time?

Do you think there are too few prospective mates available, preventing you from entering into a healthy love relationship?

Do you think all men are dogs?

As a single mom, are you now tired of dating the wrong type of man over and over again?

Do you and your friends' conversations often center around your "no-good" man's/baby daddy's ridiculous behavior toward you and your child(ren)?

Are you tired of dating men who don't/can't appreciate your beauty/talents/gifts?

Do you only seem to date men with whom you are not equally yoked?

Are you ready to "level up" in your dating life to match your career success?

Do you feel unattractive, unworthy, or valueless?

Have you ever felt like you can't break through to your true potential?

Have you ever felt exploited, overlooked, ignored, or marginalized? Even worse, do you feel unappreciated, silenced, or exiled?

#SingleMomsMatter Manifesto

#SingleMomsMatter.

Single moms attract abundant love, support, and wealth. As desirable subjects, single moms possess attributes and gifts prized by the world's most successful people. Single moms, who were once subject to demonization as immoral, lazy, irresponsible, and unattractive, can now be recognized as highly valued creatives whose vital contributions have a strong impact on the world around us. Single moms represent a new way of looking at beauty, success, and strength. Although we are often under-resourced, single moms make a way out of no way, marking our ingenuity and wit. Single moms can now be recognized as resilient, disciplined leaders of nontraditional households who consistently attract their true worth. As symbols of courage and faith, the vulnerability of single moms is no longer mischaracterized as weakness. Being a single mom means rising above societal stigmas, discouragement, and discrimination, denoting great emotional strength, a loving spirit, a sacred status, and an uncommon beauty.

#SingleMomsMatter represents a "new common sense," a new standard of critical thought. Using #SingleMomsMatter, institutional changes are enacted benefitting everyone, not only a privileged few. Ranging from the individual, to an institution, to an entire society, single moms, as change agents, attract all the resources needed to share their gifts with the world. As such,

#SingleMomsMatter, transforms the way society thinks about beauty, love, work, motherhood, mastery and other ideals, thereby making our world a better place.

#SingleMomsMatter reflects a new intersectional narrative, displacing old, dominant stories in which our image and unique gifts were distorted. A new Digital Age of technology levels the playing field, ensuring single moms effectively represent ourselves using our own words. Although we must continue to challenge bullies, assholes, and loudmouths who seek to dominate the airwaves to misrepresent us, as society continues a trend of becoming more conscious, the single mom is increasingly sought out to represent ourselves including our uncommon, yet well-respected perspective.

Single moms overcome our own exhaustion, our own overwhelmed sensibilities about the seemingly insurmountable obstacles we encounter. As a result of being slandered, we face under-resourcing, under-cooperation, and a lack of mercy. Despite the hardships we face, single moms persevere to discover our true worth. Because we know our true worth, we know we can attract all the love and support we need and then some.

Beyond a "desperate housewife," #SingleMomsMatter reflects a "visionary pragmatism" that balances higher order thinking with the realities of everyday life. Single moms model an ability to think complex thoughts while keeping one's feet solidly planted on the ground. In this way, single moms model a new subject whose eyes are wide open, who is neither extreme nor reckless, an "everyday creative" par excellence.

Furthermore, by first valuing our own images, single moms do not seek attention or validation from the outside, a first step in newly and effectively representing ourselves. Our new image foregrounds our high self-worth, our ability to establish a wholesome structure as well as juggle multiple responsibilities. At the same time single moms communicate effectively with the world around us as down to earth personalities and competent contributors. Also, our new single mom image means new possibilities for love and success.

Our understanding of #SingleMomsMatter makes us increasingly attractive, especially to those who can truly mirror our worth through providing us with the love and support we deserve. The most successful individuals, organizations, and institutions alike prefer our #SingleMomsMatter insight, recognizing our intersectional perspective and power as assets for which we are beautifully rewarded.

Chapter Two

SingleMoms 101:Intro to Single Mom's Lit

I, too, married, had children, and then divorced. What's more, I was left to raise our two children alone. Ironically, my divorce made love and marriage more important to me than ever. My marriage taught me a lot about myself, and I wanted nothing more than to keep growing through a relationship. My dysfunctional relationship made me more desirous of experiencing a healthy love relationship.

I married after finishing my undergraduate degree. I returned home from college feeling confused and lacking direction. I felt pressure to be an "adult" with no idea how to do so or any emotional support to facilitate my process. Immaturity and insecurity made me unsure of my life's path. I felt pressured to marry rather than remain single and risk being perceived as "unattractive." It was a bad place from which to enter a love relationship, but I didn't know any better. I mistakenly thought marriage might provide a stability I couldn't seem to establish within myself.

My children were born during the first and last semesters of a master's degree program which directly corresponded with the beginning and ending of my marriage. Somehow, I'd managed to keep my studies up despite struggling in my marriage. For more than three years I endured the drama of a relationship that never improved despite much counseling, several separations, and too many tit-for-tat battles.

With the help of a 12 step program (Codependents Anonymous), I finally accepted my marriage as unredeemable. As I worked the steps, I found a resolve to leave my then husband, thereby putting my own emotional, physical, and material needs first. For the first time, I took 100% responsibility for my happiness rather than depending on a societal institution, in this case marriage, as the main source of my identity. Instead of buying into a story in which power was centered outside myself, I refocused my vision on my life purpose, an undertaking which had never before failed me as a source of strength. In fact, being in touch with my heart's desire had previously saved my life on several occasions. Although I'd forsaken my purpose to enter into a marriage unsupportive of it, I would never make such a mistake again.

As a new divorcee in my late 20s, fresh out of a University of California master's degree program, I was still unclear about what direction in which I was headed. My graduate degree represented a dream come true since it was in a field I loved. However, I was jobless and broke, having no one to turn to for financial or emotional support. My two children, at 3 years old and 18 months were bright lights in my life, full of love and energy; however, I wasn't sure how I would face all of the challenges of raising them alone. For example, the cost of childcare for two preschoolers was an expense that was hard enough for two people to cover; now, I had to figure out how to manage the arrangements and the expenses without any help.

I wasn't, in fact, looking forward to covering any of my household expenses alone. Truth be told, money management wasn't my strong suit. My ex-husband and I never developed a money management system together (probably contributing to the downfall of our marriage), so

I still didn't have much quality experience. For me, money was an abstract, overwhelming idea. I was both fascinated and confused by it. Mostly, I had a scarcity mentality. I was always worried about not having enough money. However, in spite of my focus on lack and limitation, I regularly challenged myself to be fearless in the face of the unknown. At this point, the unknown variable I faced was from where the financial and emotional support to raise my children alone would come?

I'd picked up a scarcity mentality along my life's journey. Although I believed in education as an ideal, I'd had very few models of how to apply what I knew to achieve financial abundance. Although "money wisdom" was passed down to me through sayings like "pay yourself first" and "don't sweat the small stuff," my day-to-day examples were those of lack and limitation, and, at times, even desperation. By the time I was an adult, I was really confused about money, especially how to manage it and acquire wealth.

It was a bold move to leave my husband and go it alone, but I did so with desires of a happy life. However, I did not have a clear vision of exactly what I wanted my new life to look like. On one hand, I moved forward with big hopes and expectations; on the other hand, my lack of vision made my scarcity mentality my default mindset. Consequently, my movement often looked like one step forward and two steps back.

For example, upon completing my first graduate degree from the top public school in the country, I didn't try to pursue a Ph.D. at a comparable school. Against the advice of my most valued mentor, I didn't seek out admissions to top schools in the country. I settled for a second choice school under the guise that any Ph.D. was better than no

Ph.D. My scarcity mentality kicked in, and I couldn't see the advantages of going to a better university. I could not see the ways settling for less would negatively affect my career. Little did I know my vision was clouded by my fears.

My scarcity mentality led me to settle for mediocrity rather than strive for my best. I'd often repeated the saying "if you shoot for the moon, you will always land among the stars," but I forgot to remember its call to excellence. Admittedly, I felt sorry for myself because of my situation as a single mom. When I looked around for support and found none, I felt betrayed. I was still making the mistake of looking outside of myself for validation. When I didn't get the support I thought I deserved, I took it out on myself instead of questioning those who were unable to see my value. I held myself back as a way of trying to fit in. Even though I should have been used to it by then, standing out still scared me.

In truth, I was afraid of my own power. I suffered from a fear Marianne Williamson referred to in her most famous words, "Our deepest fear is not that we are inadequate. Our deepest fear is that we are powerful beyond measure. It is our Light, not our Darkness, that most frightens us." Fear of making my dreams come true held me back. I was a perfectionist. I was afraid of making mistakes lest I fail. Failure, in my messed up thinking, was not something I could overcome. I was hypersensitive about being set up by others for failure. I didn't wholly trust authority or society to point me in a direction that was in my best interest.

Although I was now unsure of myself, my own power, my true Self, was not completely unknown to me. I had previously exercised my personal power at age 12 and a half when, without help from an adult, I fully orchestrated a cross country move for myself and my younger sister by one year and two days. In other words, with my sister in tow, I secretly escaped from my mother's abusive Ohio home to live with my father in California. I did so as a way of taking full responsibility for my sister and my well-being since my mother suffered from an undiagnosed illness, Grave's disease, which made her incapable of our care.

After my parents divorced when I was about two, my mother retained primary custody despite her condition for which mental illness was a symptom. Even worse, her second husband moved us to Ohio where he continued to physically and emotionally abuse us. After many unsuccessful appeals to her, I decided to act on my own and my sister's behalf. I executed a secret plan to get my sister and myself out of her house. Although I risked my mother's and stepfather's ire and retaliation, I knew that remaining in their house was a bigger risk, a risk to my physical and mental well-being, my life even. Due to our isolation from any extended family who we'd left in California, I had little outside validation that my well-being mattered to anyone else, but I made my runaway plan anyway. Little did I know that through the elements through which I executed my plan—self-care, goal setting/planning, silence, and faith—I had created a success blueprint for myself that I could refer to ever after.

Chapter Three

Runaway Love

"Nothing else to do but get her clothes and pack…" *Runaway Love* (2007), Ludacris Ft. Mary J. Blige

My runaway from my mother's home at age 12 was months in the making. It required the planning and execution of any full scale stage or movie production. I facilitated all communication, secured all necessary permissions, coordinated all departures and arrivals. I even remained calm once we arrived at our new destination and my father was so late to pick us up that the airline threatened to send us back. What's worse, while living through these moments, I could not discuss the details of the plan with anyone, not even my sister, lest they panic and call the whole thing off. In my silence, I remained singularly focused, relying solely on belief in my plan and my faith in God.

My ability to plan my runaway resulted from years of extensive reading as well as my training in ballet and gymnastics. I confidently hatched my escape after reading as much children's literature and Black authored works as I could get my hands on. Despite my tender age, I read all of the books Maya Angelou had written up until that point and my favorites, such as Rosa Guy, Walter Dean Meyers, V.C. Andrews, Judy Blume, Mildred Taylor, and others too numerous to list here. In the process of reading nearly every book in the children's section of the library along with many of my favorite African American authors, I developed a love for culture and wisdom. Furthermore, I could easily relate to confusion or helplessness child subjects endured as they moved through a world that didn't make much sense. I empathized with my literary heroines' imperiled choices. I critically examined antagonists' manipulations. A villain's desperate decisions taught me what NOT to do, helping me to avoid some of the drama resulting from poor choices. My literacy coupled with a physical strength, habit of choreography, and sense of grace gave me enough presence of mind to devise a getaway plan. My dancing and gymnastics performance experience provided me with enough courage to carry my plan out.

I can barely remember the day my sister and I left. I think there were about six months between the time I called my dad asking him if we could come live with him and the day we boarded a plane from Columbus to Los Angeles. By the time we departed, I was so in the habit of acting "normal," as if a major change in our lives wasn't about to happen, I didn't even have to work hard to curb my enthusiasm. By the time we left, I'd coolly asked my mom if we could live with my dad (since, obviously, he'd said yes), finished my ninth grade year while running track, and refrained from indulging in ANY conversation with my sister about our move since she was sure to mention my excitement to my mom. Not talking to my sister about the getaway play was the hardest part of my cool act since I liked to share everything with her. Once on the West coast, I had to keep my cool act up so as not to overwhelm my father with my problems, lest he'd send me back. Not to worry. By the time we reached him, my getaway plan and celebration of its successful execution was buried deep within my heart, not to return for at least 20 years.

I was in a safer living situation with my father, but the physical and emotional abuse and neglect I'd suffered had taken its toll. Even worse, I couldn't talk about what I'd been through, which made therapeutic dialogue impossible. I was happy to live with my Dad, but I felt ugly, unworthy of love, and worthless inside. I missed my mom terribly, but I knew living with her was impossible. I felt lost and alone.

Despite my emotional pain, I held an abiding belief in myself within my heart. Even though I wasn't clear of my place in the world, my heart contained a faith and deep knowledge of my ability to produce life changing results. My deep-seated confidence was one reason my bad feelings did not overtake me. By running away from my mother's home to my father's care, I had significantly changed my life's circumstances. Now that I'd achieved such an accomplishment, my spirit could not easily be diminished.

Somehow, I knew, even as a young teenager, there were larger pitfalls in life I had to avoid, pitfalls that had nothing to do with me as an individual, yet threatened me still. For better or worse, no one warned me against these pitfalls or seemed to want to help me avoid them. In this way, I felt set up to fail, which frustrated me. I was especially sensitive about negative images others projected onto me depicting me as unreliable, a "problem child," or dependent before I even had a chance to express my talents! My self-image did not correspond with any of these characterizations, and I was determined not to buy into them.

Although I knew what I did not want to be, I struggled to find images that I could emulate. I had a very hard time trusting authority figures; I questioned everything, especially instances in which I perceived injustice and/or ignorance. Unfortunately, few comforting answers were forthcoming. In the era of my childhood, resources for such issues as women's rights, teenage runaways, child exploitation, abuse, and neglect were not so visible. In fact, these phrases weren't even commonly used. My subject position as a displaced, young woman of color was routinely demonized, even though I was not fully responsible. Outside of the books I continued to read and God's grace, I had very few resources to consult when navigating through the world. I had a very tough time making sense of things. I was creative, but did not yet know how to apply my talents in a constructive way. I encountered many discouragements. However, I am thankful that I did not suffer more adversity than I did! At age 16, I graduated high school and left home for college.

Throughout young adulthood, my self-image swung back and forth between confident and insecure. I had a problem communicating, which was undoubtedly tied to my getaway secret. By this time, my secret was buried deep in my heart where I was unable to access and be fully strengthened by it. I worked hard to develop my image, but a complete picture remained elusive without this key information. I sought a stable identity, a tremendous challenge for young women like me who are subject to many (intersectional even) pressures with very little support. However, I was committed to finding my way through studying, truth telling, and spiritual practice. I cultivated my relationship with my Higher Power even as I enjoyed college life. All the while, I struggled to figure out my core beliefs through which I could effectively express myself.

My "secrets to success," embedded deep in my heart since my getaway, fueled me without my conscious input. My getaway made me a purpose driven, results oriented young woman. Once I decided on a goal, I let nothing deter me. Consequently, I earned bachelor and (later) master degrees in fields I love. Like many other African American women before me, including many who were also single moms, I empowered myself through education, using it as a means of imagining myself in new ways. Education, in fact, proves to be a crucial factor in transforming the lives of women all over the world. However, we can still struggle with believing in ourselves since images of educated women in society take a backseat to other, more dominant images of women. In spite of discouraging cultural policy, single moms are good to remember wisdom imparted by Booker T. Washington, a former slave who became an orator, political advisor, and founder of a private educational institution (among many other achievements), of which he states, "Success is not measured by the heights one attains, but by the heights one overcomes in its attainment." I would not always remember Washington's edict; I accomplished my goals, but I still struggled with a clear self-image and the self-confidence that comes with it.

Fast forward to my divorce when I was just beginning to believe in my own light again. My life's path was largely illuminated through my spiritual practice as well as by accomplishing my formal educational goals. Now, it was time to bring knowledge and wisdom together. Like my getaway plan, it was time to successfully execute a bigger dream for myself. This time, my children and I would move forward from a non-normative position as a single mom headed household. Thankfully, I unquestioningly believed in my post-divorce plan the same way I had no doubts about my getaway plan when I left my mother's house.

Follow up questions:

1. Have you identified, mourned, and overcome remains of your childhood that affect your communication with yourself and others?
   A. Did you go through 5 stages of grief (denial, anger, bargaining, depression and acceptance) to fully mourn what you missed in childhood? If not, make a plan to do so.

   B. Have you, as a child or as an adult, taken 100% responsibility for your situation?

   C. What results can you use as evidence for your answer?

2. Who are your favorite authors/artists?

   A. How can they inspire your journey as a SingleMom?

3. Do you maintain your own privacy by keeping your plans to yourself?

4. Describe an instance in which you planned and executed something without telling anyone else beforehand.

5. What is your Big Picture Plan?

Chapter Four

#SingleMomMagic

My divorce broke my heart, driving me to seek solutions to my personal development, communication, and LoveLife issues. Once I left my husband, I moved to a new city to make a new life. Although I decided to do so, I did not have a clear plan, especially with regard to my new LoveLife status as a young divorcee. All was not lost since, from my marriage, I had learned some valuable lessons. I used my marriage as a mirror, reflecting to me my strengths and weakness. I now had data, tools, and structures to create my ideal life. I was determined to make my dreams come true, especially with regard to my career, financial, and relationship goals. As had been my habit since childhood, I first sought understanding of my new status as a single mom through reading.

Lucky for me, my love of reading not only helped me get away from my mother's house, but it also saw me through high school and my undergraduate degree in History. Next, I mapped a path for my career as a cultural producer, a path fueled by my graduate studies. I pursued my passion for storytelling by completing a Master of Arts in Folklore and then pursuing a Ph.D. in Communications Studies with an emphasis in Performance Studies. While reading for graduate studies assignments, I read many, many, many references on love and dating from psychological, cultural, and anthropological angles. Additionally, spiritual scholars, such as, Wayne Dyer, Iyanla Vanzant, Marianne

Williamson, and Deepak Chopra, remained, as always, in heavy rotation on my reading list. Following my divorce, I even began (and enjoyed) checking out what pop culture experts said about dating. I was informed and amused by "dating do and don't" lists pervading popular advice books, magazine articles, and television shows. I examined dating from the points of views of both men and women, and I learned a lot! For the first time in my life, I was enjoying my process of self-awareness and development.

Since I lived in married student housing, I was also able to observe the marriages of my neighbors and colleagues. I saw that I wasn't the only one that was still learning and growing. In fact, I've heard that as many as 75% of married graduate students end their marriages. Finally, I stopped beating myself up and blaming my childhood issues for my divorce. As a child of divorce, I habitually traced issues I had in my marriage back to my parents' marriage. I was finally learning to accept myself for who I was, flaws and all.

Luckily, through my graduate studies, I studied communication skills on many levels. I developed my interpersonal, intercultural, group communication, and even my performing skills. I became more flexible, more aware of interactional give and take. For all my hard work at school, I was awarded a departmental fellowship. Outward validation was not the goal, but it still felt great!

I slowly began to understand my position as a single mom as a blessing in disguise, a heroic subject position. I increasingly recognized my single mom status as a reflection of my Sacred Self, a holiness within. As a single mom I had an opportunity to realize my best self, exercise my faith, (finally) take care of myself in a way that I deserved, and pursue my dreams. My abilities to prioritize my well-being, establish boundaries with others, and visualize my success, abilities I'd developed from running away as an adolescent, were gifts, not curses. What's more, as a single mom, I interrupted destructive generational patterns, establishing healthy routines all while learning from my past mistakes. Examples of these patterns include staying in a dysfunctional relationship to avoid raising children alone or to maintain appearances, as well as abandoning my preadolescent children. Since I wasn't the only one affected by my decisions, I let the high stakes involved in making healthy choices for my children and myself inspire me to a better performance. I wanted my children to learn to make their own best decisions. In my mind, the best way to ensure their good decision making was to model good decision making as much as possible. Through my struggles, my children saw me choose well, as well as execute getaways from poor decisions. Because of both my good and bad decisions, I laid groundwork for my children's empowerment through my own.

In seeking my true destiny, I came to understand my story as a single mom as a basis for my image. My story was not accurately reflected in popular images, including those propagated by government policymakers who demonized single moms as lazy, welfare abusers. Such depictions were images with which I identified in no way. On the contrary, my position as a single mom was based upon my willingness to accept 100% responsibility for my circumstances as well as cut my losses in a bad situation. As a single mom, I was called to heal myself, making transformation my ideal action as opposed to "winning" or marriage. Not only did I get in touch with forgotten aspects of my story, I got in touch with my innocence, joy and desires. What's more, I became okay with the fact that few images projected around me would accurately represent or mirror me. This realization did not dishearten me as I realized a freedom in reimagining myself, in refashioning my own image. Furthermore, I now understood my self-image as created through my actions, not through my or anyone else's words. I now looked at myself through a lens of my story and did not feel guilt, shame, or anger about the image I saw.

Less Talk, More Action

My graduate program and my children kept me very busy. My reading and writing assignments, part time jobs and now elementary school aged children meant a calendar full of activity. The funny thing was, the busier I got, the more I longed for a relationship. Implementing all that I learned was tough. I must be honest; at first, I was unwilling to sacrifice my desire for a LoveLife for my career goals. In these moments, I acted neurotically. In other words, I tried to have my cake and eat it too. With unproductive results, I tried to focus on both my graduate studies and my love life at the same time. It was relatively early in my journey as a single mom, but I was discouraged by a lack of progress in my love life. I couldn't understand why I had yet to meet a man who was right for me? I was doing all the things I thought were right, so what was the problem?

Even though I was working hard, I wasn't working smart enough. I had yet to achieve an ultimate focus and clarity. Now, not only was I missing a relationship, my studies were starting to suffer. I couldn't focus enough to make significant progress on my dissertation. My exhaustion was getting the best of me. I couldn't see how I was going to finish the Ph.D. program, get a good job, and continue to solely support my family. I was backsliding down a slippery slope into indecision and a scarcity mentality.

Admittedly, I was deeply discouraged. After a certain point, I couldn't seem to make headway in my degree program, but I couldn't figure out what was wrong. I had not yet attracted a love with whom I could build a life. I needed a game changer, but I couldn't figure out what was needed. I was overwhelmed, disappointed, and lacking faith. Emotionally, I'd hit rock bottom. I was spent.

I felt like a failure. First, my marriage broke up, and now, the big risk I took to achieve my dream goal of earning a Ph.D. looked like it wasn't going to work out. As I did with regard to my scarcity mentality, I had to face another fear; this time, I realized it was fear of success. I'd courageously embarked upon my journey, but I was not engaged in practices that would ensure my success. I was not doing what was necessary to finish my degree. Since I was in the habit of taking 100% responsibility for my life situations, I had to ask myself, "Am I purposely sabotaging my own success?"

After thinking about it, I had to admit that one of the biggest mistakes I made was talking too much.

"Show, Don't Tell"- (Becoming a "Meta Mama")

My new life as a single mom made me feel more isolated than ever before. I was confused and overwhelmed. My feelings were exacerbated by my graduate work. Ultimately, writing a dissertation is a lonely endeavor. To compensate, I would talk about my feelings to those with whom I thought I could trust. At the time, I naively thought other people were consciously engaged in the same type of transformational journey as I; therefore, I thought, like me, they would appreciate company. Even worse, I thought I could trust others with my feelings and ideas, so I opened up to share. BIG MISTAKE! It took a couple of instances of deep betrayal before I fully realized that talking about my thoughts and feelings was not the best way to handle them. Little did I know that these conversations were not held in confidence. When I found out my privacy was not a priority, I was devastated. I had to deal with the hard fact that my talks were not a source of love and acceptance for which I looked. At first, I thought my predicament a lonely place to be; however, through these disappointments, I learned to love and accept myself first and the love of others would follow.

Also, I realized talking too much actually pushed my success further from me. Talking was a nervous habit I engaged in distracting me from my center. Talking too much was the opposite of being mindful and only ended up making me feel more confused. Here, I could be reminded of a key lesson that ensured the success of my getaway plan more than twenty years before: ***In order to ensure the success of your plans, tell no one.***

"Talk is cheap" is a common saying reflecting this wisdom. Talking too much gives others the wrong impression; it says we do not value ourselves. Consequently, those to whom you talk too much never perceive your true value. Those who engage in this bad habit suffer since, in the words of Maya Angelou, "Whining is not only graceless, it can be dangerous. It can alert a brute that a victim is in the neighborhood." When we talk too much we can inadvertently give others permission to treat us poorly. In the case of a single mom, by extension, we give brutes permission to treat our children poorly, as well.

Nonverbal communication makes up 70% of our communication. If we want to project an effective image of ourselves, talking is not a lasting way to do it. Unfortunately, people have a way of using your words against you no matter what you say. When you talk to others, you must know your audience to avoid either "casting your pearls to swine," having others rip off your ideas, or both! Talking can be a form of procrastination. Talking can be a waste of precious time that could be better spent taking direct action. I misused it as a way of getting in my own way. Instead of writing, I talked, slowing my progress toward realizing my goals.

My graduate studies helped me practice many modes of communication. I set out to communicate in the most effective ways, ensuring I was treated well by others. Through my studies, I learned the phrase, "show, don't tell," an motto often used by actors. I found it to be an effective mindset to maintain, especially when communicating to others my sense of self-worth. Instead of trying to convince them of my worth through words, I communicate through my actions.

"Say What is Good or Keep Silent"

Once I admitted talking too much was costing me the very success I so desired, I took responsibility for my negative feelings, loneliness, fear, and failure. I gave up trying to get others to understand me as a way of seeking love. I meditated on wisdoms tied to communication and success, such as, "you have two ears and one mouth which means you should listen twice as much as you talk" as well as my favorite, "say what is good or keep silent." "Silence is golden" ties the practice to an aesthetic as well as a material value, which appealed to me very much since I wanted to be thought of as both beautiful and worthy, like a precious stone or a work of art. Instead of more talking, I spent more time thinking about what I truly wanted for myself and making it happen.

In earnest, I resumed my spiritual practices and even sought out others. I instituted more rituals of prayer, writing, exercise, meditation, yoga, and Pilates. I took my children to many local natural springs and pools, enjoying spending time with them in nature. I located my center from which I called what I wanted into being.

Even though I felt alone, I eliminated unloving, unsupportive, and unbalanced relationships. I severely limited time with those who didn't value my company or who downright abused my attention.

What's more, I refused to play into a "keep up with the Joneses" mentality perpetuated by upwardly mobile neighbors or parents of my children's playmates. I began journaling in earnest, cataloging my ideas for use in later creative acts. I became my own best friend, searching my heart with deep questions and finding satisfaction in the answers I found there. Above all, I refrained from judging myself harshly and tried to be as gentle and loving with myself as possible. I refrained from working so hard to fix myself, relishing in just being myself. I accepted myself fully and did not try to convince anyone else of their need to do so. I saved myself a lot of energy that I redirected into self-care and other activities I enjoyed.

Order and Organization

Another thing I figured out in graduate school was the success I desired required my willingness to relinquish order as society proscribed it. This was actually perfect since trying to fit into society's boxes didn't seem to work out well for me anyway. I now understood that I had to create my own order, which meant I now had a good excuse not to represent myself as an ideal "soccer mom."

The order upon which my world was based would reinforce my personal ideals: education, peace, art, justice, love, etc. I set about creating an order reproducing my ideals within my personal life, as well.

My goal was to manage all areas of my life, setting a good example for my children to achieve a "wholesome discipline," as referenced in Max Ehrmann's 1929 poem, "Desiderata."

Desiderata

Go placidly amid the noise and haste,
and remember what peace there may be in silence.
As far as possible without surrender
be on good terms with all persons.
Speak your truth quietly and clearly;
and listen to others,
even the dull and the ignorant;
they too have their story.
Avoid loud and aggressive persons,
they are vexations to the spirit.
If you compare yourself with others,
you may become vain and bitter;
for always there will be greater and lesser persons than
        yourself.
Enjoy your achievements as well as your plans.
Keep interested in your own career, however humble;
it is a real possession in the changing fortunes of time.

Exercise caution in your business affairs;
for the world is full of trickery.
But let this not blind you to what virtue there is;
many persons strive for high ideals;
and everywhere life is full of heroism.
Be yourself.

Especially, do not feign affection.
Neither be cynical about love;
for in the face of all aridity and disenchantment
it is as perennial as the grass.

Take kindly the counsel of the years,
gracefully surrendering the things of youth.
Nurture strength of spirit to shield you in sudden
        misfortune.
But do not distress yourself with dark imaginings.
Many fears are born of fatigue and loneliness.
Beyond a wholesome discipline,
be gentle with yourself.

You are a child of the universe,
no less than the trees and the stars;
you have a right to be here.
And whether or not it is clear to you,
no doubt the universe is unfolding as it should.

Therefore be at peace with God,
whatever you conceive Him to be,
and whatever your labors and aspirations,
in the noisy confusion of life keep peace with your soul.

With all its sham, drudgery, and broken dreams,
it is still a beautiful world.
Be cheerful.
Strive to be happy.

Keeping the "Desiderata's" wisdom in my heart, I set about structuring my life in a way that would facilitate happiness and success, including effective communication with the world around me.

Reordering my priorities included shifts such as:

1. Organizing my life so that my overhead is low and self-care maintenance is high.
2. Communicating with others in a way that boundaries are clear and I "teach others how to treat me" (Dr. Phil).
3. Establishing high standards and ground rules for my life so as not to be easily influenced.
4. Establishing a healthy structure for the household so children feel safe yet confident.
5. Taking 100% responsibility for childcare so as not to feel desperate for help from a prospective mate.

Clearing the Clutter

As a part of establishing a healthy structure in my household, I set about cleaning up my house, especially with regard to simplifying my household.

I needed to get rid of all the things I couldn't immediately use. Since, upon my move to Texas, I'd downsized from a spacious, Spanish Mediterranean home on a California hill to a two-bedroom military style apartment, I had a lot of extra furniture and belongings for which I didn't have space. In fact, I think I even paid for a storage unit for a couple of years. However, once I made up my mind to declutter, I wasted no time dealing with it. I sold a dining table and 6 chairs for next to nothing to a lucky family who lived across the parking lot. Finally, I swallowed my pride and asked a colleague, Terri, to come help me clean and organize. She was a regular drill sergeant when it came to throwing out my clutter; she didn't tolerate my stories about all the crap I'd accumulated. In fact, I'm pretty sure she threw away a lot of stuff without even telling me so as not to have to hear my mouth. In essence, even though I'd left my marriage, I was still attached to things we had accumulated during it. Finally, I was detaching from my belongings that I used to feel stable. I could now open myself to new possibilities, new opportunities, new ways of being.

The good news was I had everything I needed to get organized; I just needed help in implementing it. Terri and I put to use all the magazine holders, file cabinets, and book shelves I had but wasn't using. She helped me clean out my closets and organize my shoes, clothes, and jewelry. When we finished, I felt so much more hopeful. Terri, the children, and I celebrated with a high-energy party to which we invited our close friends and colleagues.

Now that I'd worked on my living environment, it was easier to organize other areas of my life. I began to implement calendaring and sought out other means of managing my time better. I must admit, I was a night owl and loved to stay up late. It was a horrible habit considering the kids woke up early and their dad wasn't there to help, but I slugged along, getting better bit by bit as time went on. Some of my time management issues were tied to a habit of procrastination. As I identified these problem areas, acknowledged them, and asked for help in dealing with them, I got better and better.

For the first time in my life, I began workouts at a gym. Since I was a full time graduate student, my university gym membership fees were included in the tuition I paid every semester. I even went beyond my basic membership to hire a student trainer who created a workout routine that I've used for some ten years afterward. I integrated trips to the gym into my weekly schedule. My energy level went up. I loved watching my body change as my workouts continued. My clothes fit differently, and I gained more confidence in my appearance. Slowly but surely, I was getting better at handling my life as a single mom. The structure I implemented gave me the support I needed when I felt I had nowhere else to turn. My fears dissipated, and I became less anxious. Most importantly, my vision became clearer. As in the case of the clutter I'd cleared from my house, my increased energy could now be directed toward my making my dreams come true.

An "Abundant Academic"™

One reference that also proved highly useful in my new life was that of my now ex-mother-in-law who, unlike my parents, worked a blue-collar job, yet had more financial freedom than they seemed to have as professionals. She traveled frequently, bought my children gifts regularly, and had access to financial resources whenever she needed them. During my marriage, she and I talked all the time about managing a household and life in general. From her, I learned a value in living beneath your means. After our numerous conversations, I better understood my maternal grandparents' example of paying their bills on time and never running up a lot of unnecessary debt. My grandparents lived in the same two-plus-bedroom, one bath house they'd purchased when my mother was a small child. They, too, lived within their means, were never desperate or focused on what they didn't have, yet lived a rich life filled with a sense of high quality.

I thought a lot about these models as I moved into my new life as a single mom. Since I had some understanding of living beneath my means, I made it a goal to keep my overhead low. In doing so, I could alleviate anxious feelings about keeping a roof over our heads and food on the table. I understood my status as a student as one of sacrifice. However, I wanted stability for my children, so I didn't want to put myself in an insecure living situation.

Thankfully, living in student housing meant reduced rent which helped to manage my many fears about the "costs of living." While I worked on my advanced degree, I wouldn't have to pay the rent at full current market value. This was especially helpful since, in our household, there was only one paycheck.

Once we moved into student housing, I deeply valued living in a convenient location among fellow students. My children always had ready playmates. In fact, if you ask them today, they would say they had an idyllic childhood.

One way I showed my appreciation was by paying my bills on time. I remember changing my mindset about bill paying from one of dread and anxiety to one of gratitude. Every time I wrote out a check to pay a bill, I would express gratitude ("thank God") that I could pay it. I now focused on what I had instead of what I didn't. I was practicing the Truth, "what you focus on expands." Such a small shift in my perspective caused a monumental shift in how I interacted with the world. I could now enter into my relationships from a place of abundance, not scarcity.

Another way of thinking about my new mindset was through the spiritual practice of gratitude. Ironically, it was through gratitude that I found my way to abundant thinking. I'd finally found my way to appreciating what I had so I could get more of what I wanted. I also learned not to fear what I didn't have. With regard to financially providing for my children, I focused on scripture admonishing believers not to fear poverty since God provides for children. It is upon this faith that I moved in confidence in financially supporting my children alone.

Once I cultivated an abundant mindset in myself, I was able to share my experience with others. I remember having a conversation with a friend from college who, having recently become a single mom herself, agonized over her finances. I advised her about having an abundant mindset, especially with regard to not wasting too much time chasing after her baby's father trying to get him to contribute regularly since that was working hard, not smart. Once we talked about the importance of focusing on things she could control rather than things she couldn't, she shifted her attention to her own career and managing what she had rather than worrying about what she didn't have. To this day, she still thanks me for helping her see her situation in a new way.

#SingleMomMagic

Now that I began to focus on what I had instead of what I didn't, I began to speak and act differently. What's more, I was able to attract the resources I needed instead of repelling them due to fear. In a word, gratitude improved my attitude which improved my altitude. Not only did I give thanks for everything I had materially, I counted the blessings of unseen gifts, such as, my breath, my heartbeat, the blood flowing through my veins, and my functioning internal organs. In learning to be grateful for simple things, I could truly appreciate the (relatively) big things.

What were some of these big things? Throughout graduate school I always earned a salary. It was a graduate student's salary, but a salary nonetheless. With my salary and benefits, I paid my living expenses, was able to get new stylish glasses every year, and paid down overdue credit card bills. I practiced living within my means while making goals, visualizing my desires, and moving with inspired action. Consequently, I didn't have to be too dependent on one source of income since I could have faith that when one graduate student job ended, I could secure other, better paying positions. I attracted one opportunity after the next, effectively balancing both my studies and my household. By the time I was hired for my first tenure track faculty position, I was able to buy my very first brand new car!

Creative Power

With purpose, clarity, and more discipline in place, I could now confidently exercise my creative power. After much meditation, study, and self-care, I learned to value my own creative contributions, tracing them back to my escape from my mother's house. For the first time in almost 25 years, I was able to recall and openly discuss running away at 12 years old. I could finally recognize my story for what it was, a Black-girl-hero tale. Contrary to popular fairy tales, no Prince Charming came to rescue me; I saved my own Black-girl-child self! Interestingly, the details of my getaway story were lost on those who were closest to it. Even when I reviewed them with some of my family, they couldn't seem to make sense of the implications of my actions: I, a preadolescent without any adult's help, removed my sister and myself out of harm's way. A few even got angry with me for making them look bad! Ultimately, I had to praise God and accept myself for getting my sister and myself out of a dangerous environment since no one else would ever really celebrate with me. I accepted myself fully, my weaknesses as well as my strengths. For me, self-acceptance was not only embracing my shadow self, but I could now openly love my successes, which included my most heroic acts. In doing so, I forgave my parents for what they could not do for my sister and me, specifically, protect us from those who would do us harm. As a responsible adult, I could recognize their struggles as human beings who did the best they could. I appreciate my parents (including grandparents, aunts and uncles, and other parental figures) for giving me life, as well as for sharing with me the best they had to offer, including a quality education and early art lessons.

Accepting my success was key to executing my creative voice, a voice I'd diminished during the time I kept my runaway plans secret. In acknowledging my story, I broke through to a new creativity I was now able to exercise through my class assignments, degree requirements, and even my dissertation. My creative power facilitated an achievement of my personal, as well as my professional, goals. Eventually, my creative confidence would be channeled into creating the first ever theatre and performance studies academic program in my university's 120-year history, as well as my own digital and media production company.

Even better, my creative empowerment served me in other ways:

I developed my personal style in dress, manner, and communication. I infused "design" into my everyday life, helping me to become more prepared and attractive.

I brainstormed creative and business ideas regularly. I used Julia Cameron's *The Artist Way* as a workbook to help me recover and develop my creative self.

I claimed a new authority in the way I moved through the world. I stopped questioning myself so much and didn't ask other people's opinions or seek their approval on decisions I made.

As much as possible, I tried to be present and awake. I finally believed in myself as well as my ability to produce results that mattered, whether others could acknowledge the value of them or not.

Coupled with an understanding that the best use of my creative skills was in seeking to be most "useful to society," my goals were clearer than ever. With this new perspective, I was ready to move forward into a new leg of my spiritual journey.

Follow up questions:

1. Have you simplified your life as much as possible, especially with regard to organization, time, money, and emotions?

2. How old do you want to be when you retire? How much money do you need to retire? Work backwards to figure out your financial goals and come up with a plan for achieving them.

3. What's your single mom creative power?

    1. How do you express it?

    2. Do you regularly practice it? Why or why not?

Chapter Five

LoveMeLessons

"When someone tells you who they are, believe them."
Maya Angelou

"When you see crazy coming, cross the street." Iyanla
Vanzant

Listening (Not Looking) for Love

My view of love and dating also shifted as I became more grateful and mindful. Initially, I was very nervous about re-entering the dating world. My perfectionism held me back as I worried about all the wrong things: Would I ever love again? Little did I know, these issues were the least of my concerns, as I soon found out, my dating issues had little to do with meeting "Mr. Right," but more to do with seeing myself in my best light and attracting my best love to me. At the time, I still could not see myself clearly, so I still made the mistake of putting my focus in the wrong places.

It took me a couple of years to date after divorce. I was positively preoccupied with setting myself and my kids up for success. As in the case of my secret runaway, I built my new foundation with an end in mind. I did not look to others for easy solutions to my newfound single-mom-headed-household economy or loneliness. Therefore, I put dating on a back burner so as not to rush into anything before I was ready.

When I finally resumed dating, I focused on improving my communication skills, especially listening. I actively listened to learn everything I needed to know about a potential mate. Instead of being quick to talk about myself, I asked follow-up questions when dates talked about themselves. I mirrored their statements, summarized them, or asked them to tell me more. Even further, I did not try to interpret what they said or think of ways I could change them. If an attractive companion told me that he was not ready for a committed relationship, I took him at his word. I wasted no breath trying to convince him to change his mind, nor did I waste my time imagining a life together (not too much time anyway).

I remember a friend setting me up with her boyfriend's really cute co-worker. He was very nice and sweet (and did I mention cute?), and we talked on the phone a few times before going to see a movie together. Just when I was really beginning to enjoy his company, he told me that he was ambivalent about dating a woman with children. In his mind, my situation came with unwanted drama (i.e. baby daddy) and the possibility of breaking my children's hearts if we didn't work out. Although I didn't have any baby daddy drama (my children's absent father lived 2000 miles away) and I really wanted to get to know him better, I didn't try to convince him otherwise; choosing instead to respect his rationale. I let go of any expectations our relationship would develop. I did not take his hesitation (too) personally. In doing so, I learned that disappointment was not the end of the world. I could even appreciate the experience, especially since, as black feminist writer Alice Walker says, "The way forward is with a broken heart." Instead of internalizing my broken-heartedness, I let it propel me forward toward my love destiny.

In addition to taking a man at his word, I was also careful to listen for other signals indicating a potential mate's emotional (un)availability, mental stability, and sense of responsibility. I, again, reviewed warning signs of abusive personalities and kept them uppermost in my mind as I got to know him. When I heard something that raised a red flag in my consciousness, I immediately disqualified him as a potential mate. Since I'd left an unhealthy relationship behind when I divorced, I definitely did not want to enter into another! I knew the best way to get out of a bad situation was to avoid entering into one in the first place.

LoveMeLessons

As I harbored a crush on a date who didn't feel the same way I did, I discovered why *unrequited love*, or love that is not reciprocated, is the basis of so much poetry and art. As such, I used my love feelings to enter a creative space. I let my strong emotion enchant me. I lost myself in fantasy, composing my own poetry and prose to mark the occasions. Instead of focusing on him, I focused on the wonderful feeling, using it as a jumping off point for gauging my own happiness. Instead of looking for someone else to help me access it, I used my feelings to become clear on what loving myself felt like. I identified, edified, and satisfied my own desires. Instead of judging my fantasies, I, alone, safely explored them. In doing so, I was able to confront and vanquish any guilt or shame about what I truly liked and desired. I also became confident through my understanding of loving myself, making my communication with others clearer. I now call these communication exercises LoveMeLessons. Through my LoveMeLessons, I made a most important discovery: I learned that LOVE is not a possession attained by loving another. **Love is a state of being first accomplished through self-love.**

Even further, for the first time ever, I regularly engaged in acts of radical self-love in which I loved myself no matter what everyone else around me was doing. I began to institutionalize the best practices related to my thoughts, the food I ate, and the company I kept.

Once I felt love, I held on to it and even tried to become one with it. By not ascribing love to a person, I was able to enjoy it and share it. Love, for me, reflected a state of awareness, a state of grace that I first enjoyed within myself. Later, through my creativity, I found it possible to spread love in the world around me.

Another self-enriching LoveMeLesson I developed during this time was doing something to improve myself every time I had the temptation to first focus on a prospective mate or his needs. (Of course, my children were always a priority, and I made sure to focus on our individual and collective well-beings first.) I distracted myself from too much fantasizing about prospective loves by focusing on my career goals, working out at the gym, reading books on personal development, or otherwise improving my spiritual practices. My LoveMeLessons not only helped me refocus, they ensured that every time I came into contact with my love object, I looked and felt better than ever. In other words, redirecting my focus to caring for myself was the perfect revenge on any man who was, to me, unavailable. Every time I ran into him, I showed him what he was missing.

Furthermore, I never limited myself to dating someone exclusively when there was no commitment in place. From my pre-marriage days, I remembered running into problems when I had expectations for relationships that didn't match the reality of them. After divorce, as an exercise in detachment, I did not date exclusively unless there was a commitment in place, remaining clearheaded about my dating status.

LoveMeLessons is one means by which I instituted self-care in my life, spiritually, physically, and materially. Self-care is crucial in attracting true love since, as Dr. Phil says, "We teach people how to treat us." How do we do so? By the way we treat ourselves. If we treat ourselves as afterthoughts, worthless, or disrespectfully, we can't be surprised when others follow suit. Single moms must exercise an integrity in caring for ourselves, especially since our children depend on us and we have so much to do. Plus, our kids are extensions of us, so our self-care teaches others how to treat them too. We must realize that it is not selfish to make self-care a priority so that anyone coming into our lives has a standard by which they will be judged, a standard they must maintain. It is through self-care that we actually put our standards into our bodies. We can (and should) actually train ourselves to the best life has to offer so it becomes natural. We don't even have to think about implementing our standard; our higher standard become automatic like our bodily reflexes. Anybody who cannot meet our standard is rejected without our ever having to think about it. LoveMeLessons act as our self-care insurance, protecting us against accidental lapses in judgment or reversions to bad habits. Instead of a person or money, we can fall back on our now ingrained self-care habits, including:

1. Adequate rest
2. Regular visits to the doctor(s) and dentist
3. Exercise
4. Healthy, delicious meals

5. Social interaction with those who value your company
6. Maintaining healthy boundaries
7. Journaling
8. Time spent in nature
9. Prioritizing our tasks
10. Saying no without explanation
11. Meditating
12. Reading books for pleasure and self-development
13. Investing in both self and professional development classes, conferences and seminars.

I attracted dates, and with them, gained insight about myself. I learned where I was and was not in my personal development. For example, I discovered that my specific dating dilemmas were never about attracting true love. I found that my lack of clarity in knowing what I wanted reflected itself in who I attracted. I would get what I wanted in some areas, but not in others. For example, I attracted a love who had a stable career path; however, he did not have a stable relationship with his children. I met another man who loved children, but he didn't manage his money well. I also met men who had great personalities, but their spiritual lives were underdeveloped. In each case, I reflected on how this person mirrored me in some way. How was my relationship with my children? Was I managing my money well? Was I cultivating my spiritual life or neglecting it? Out of these experiences, I developed criteria to ensure clarity in becoming what I wanted and not merely expecting others to live up to my standards. Not only did it become clear to me that I may not have been ready for the relationship I thought I wanted, but I became increasingly aware that when it came to relationships, "timing is everything." I considered a new question: even if I *was* emotionally ready for a new relationship, was it the right time?

What time is it?

As I used relationships to gain perspective about myself, I learned to look at time in new ways. I heard anecdotes about time that I began to apply to my life, such as:

"It takes 10,000 hours to become an overnight success." Malcolm Gladwell
"Ex-husbands take 10 years before they curb their anger towards you." Fellow Divorcee and resident in Austin, Texas
"40 is the old age of youth; 50 is the youth of old age." Victor Hugo
"The age of retirement will rise to age 67 for those born after 1960." National Academy of Social Insurance

I slowly began to realize that some of the mistakes that I made that would be attributed to "youth" wouldn't always be so. In other words, I realized that my bad habits of procrastination and perfectionism could negatively affect my long term goals.

First, I examined the various ways time was reflected in nature: seasons, tides and moon phases, life cycles, women's menstruation, childbirth, menopause, etc. I also thought about man's time based constructs reflected in hours, days, months, years, quarters, holidays, and rituals. I thought about how time worked in my own life, charting my successes and failures as cycles and reflecting on when I was and wasn't in sync with nature. I remembered how I entered first grade at the age of four; my school and emotional ages were not the same. Now, I tried to enjoy my graduate studies "ordeal," but I also knew I needed to prepare for what came next. I began thinking about my time in graduate school solely as a time to structure my career.

I even began to think about an impending future when, due to my age, I would no longer be able to have children. Reaching an age beyond childbearing sobered my thinking regarding remarriage and having more children. As a single mom approaching my late 30s, I had to deal with changes in my body as well as the way the world changed around me. Since it was taking so long, in my eyes, to meet the right man, I could no longer take having a bigger family for granted. Once I honestly estimated how much longer it would take to finish the Ph.D. degree and earn tenure, I began to grieve my childbearing possibilities beyond the two I already have. Ironically, my grief enabled me to become clearer about my mate choice. Dating someone who wanted more children became less of an option since I was more clear about my goals. For me this by and large, ruled younger men out.

I'd once thought of having more children as "naturally inevitable" since I was, technically, of childbearing age. Now, I thought about having more children more consciously as opposed to coming from a selfish place of wanting them as a reflection of me. As is the case of everything else in life, with regard to my ability to procreate, I could courageously apply the wisdom "this, too, shall pass."

Follow up questions:

1. How do you show yourself love?

2. What are your rituals for loving yourself?

3. Do you continue them once you've entered into a love relationship?

4. Do you regularly make mistakes in judgement, get distracted by looks, or misinterpret others' signals?

5. Do you look instead of *listen* for love? (symptoms include falling for "six pack and a smile" or a "type" over and over)?

6. What plan do you have for improving your listening skills?

7. Do you have a one-year plan? If so, what is it?

8. Do you have a three-year plan? If so, what is it?

9. Do you have a ten-year plan? If so what is it?

10. Have you created a retirement plan for yourself?

Chapter Six

Single Moms Come of Age

In the past 50 years, the rate of families headed by single mothers has tripled.[1]

According to recent statistics, households headed by single moms are a new norm. Of the 12 million single parent households in the United States, 83% of them are headed by single moms.[2] Even further, nontraditional families and households are fast becoming a new rule, especially since the summer of 2015 when the United States Supreme Court ruled same sex marriage constitutional.

Of course, such a dramatic increase in numbers is attributable to complex political, economic, and social factors, such as: a rise (and fall) of political and social movements questioning American societal structures based, in part, upon a two-parent-household model (i.e. civil rights movement, feminism, anti-Vietnam war protests, etc.); a high rate of divorce during the 1970s that made children

---

[1]

https://www.theatlantic.com/business/archive/2013/09/the-mysterious-and-alarming-rise-of-single-parenthood-in-america/279203/

[2]https://singlemotherguide.com/single-mother-statistics/

raised in divorced households more likely to go through divorce themselves; a rise in the number of working women; the stock market crashes of 1987 and 2008; the dot com and real estate bubbles of the late 1990s and early 2000s; 9/11; a rise of economic inequality in the 2000s.

Changes in the make-up of American households has been so swift, in fact, that 25 year olds today would probably not believe the uproar caused by the television image of Murphy Brown, a successful, single, career woman choosing to forgo marriage to raise a child alone. During the 1991-92 television season, Brown's image, played by Candace Bergen, not only made national headlines but even incited a response from the Vice President of the United States, sparking a nationwide debate about family values! Oh, how quickly times have changed!

Unfortunately, however, although the number of single mom headed households has greatly risen, her image still suffers from stigmas from earlier eras. In 1965, Daniel Moynihan wrote a report disparaging images of single moms, especially that of African Americans.

For more than 50 years after, images of single moms were affected.

Finally, the tide is beginning to turn. A "new era" workplace is trending towards qualities single moms embody.

Here are some other reasons why the value of single moms will continue to rise:

- Children of the "Era of Divorce" grew up, got married, had children, and divorced, not necessarily in that order. Now, their children are having children out of wedlock due, in part, to their parents' examples, as well as distrust in marriage as an institution.

- Education rates among women are rising, challenging traditional gender roles.
- "Successful" women are opting to have children without marriage.
- The median age for marriage has risen.

Furthermore, new age employers and business leaders now understand that employees are their biggest assets, not liabilities. Instead of reinforcing old models of thinking in which top down communication, rigid working schedules, corporate jargon and double standards are practiced, new business leaders value open communication, flexible working schedules, multitasking, honesty and one standard for all. Such new ways of thinking demands a reconsideration of the value of single moms. Single moms can now be appreciated as saavy, forward thinkers who facilitate transformation in the world around them.

As images of single moms increasingly become more visible, our struggles yield critical insights on personal healing and transformation. Having actively engaged in such a process, our images become references for those in need of healing, as well. Single moms are now emblematic of a struggling human being who centers herself to overcome life's challenges. As a need for nontraditional, transformational models of leadership is increasingly acknowledged, our vulnerabilities are now recognized as strengths. In a new business age, a single mom, as a leader of a nontraditional household, can be valued for her self-initiative, collaborative skills, and adaptability among other things.

Chapter Seven

#SingleMomMiracles

After more than 18 years of countless hours of study, observation, trial, error, and sacrifice, I finally attracted a love of my life!

I'm now happily partnered with a record company CEO, author, and entrepreneur who recently launched his own cosmetics company. My new boo's goals reflect billion dollar objectives, as his vision for his companies easily exceeds that mark. It is for this reason that I affectionately refer to him as my "Billionaire Boo." Even more important, he has a personal relationship with his higher power, is kind and generous, a good listener, a caring father, an excellent cook, and even a skilled masseuse! His children are all college graduates from top ranked universities; his youngest is six months older than my oldest. I'd finally broken through my dating limitations to attract a man who reflected all my best attributes and met my love life criteria.

I finally achieved my LoveLife goals! I now have a relationship with someone who doesn't reflect my old habits of "dating down," who understands, loves, and cherishes me and knows how to show it. My kids with whom I shared what I learned about dating along the way even approve!

What's the difference? How did I find a quality love relationship after so many years of disappointment and dissatisfaction?

How did I heal unbroken mental habits established in childhood?

How was I able to bring all my knowledge and experience together, manifesting a love I truly desired and deserved?

#SingleMomMastery

When I met my Billionaire Boo, I really wasn't focused on dating. My children had just left home for college, and I was exploring my new status as an empty nester. I was using my new "free time" to focus on my academic writing, have dinner with friends once a week, and avoid worrying about the kids too much. Unfortunately, I'd recently been in a head-on car collision in which I suffered a concussion. At the time I met my boo, I'd just gotten my feet back under me.

A few months before, I'd met a guy online that I thought was perfect for me! We were both college professors, had children the same age, and could talk on the phone for hours. The only problem was, he lived more than three hours away and frequently traveled around the world as a musician. My LoveMeLessons said long distance relationships were a definite no-no. This was a red flag, but I tried to be flexible since we had so much in common on paper. I stayed open to the possibilities even though it was hard to arrange to see him in person.

When he called me on a Saturday morning to ask me out to a high-profile event that very night, another red flag went up, but I agreed to go anyway. My LoveMeLessons prohibited this kind of arrangement since I knew a man that was truly interested in me would have been more considerate when taking me out, especially since we lived so far apart. Despite my misgivings, I dug through my closet and found an outfit I could be both cute and comfortable in and hurried to get dressed in the three hours it would take him to get from his house to mine. When he pulled up, I looked like a million bucks. He on the other hand, had on jeans and designer tennis shoes. I didn't take this as a third red flag, but I probably should have. Even though it was supposed to be an exciting night, my "head, heart, and gut"[3] weren't aligned on this. We weren't in Houston, but I knew we had a problem.

Long story short, the night was a mess. Curiously, even though the event started in less than two hours, my date made a 45-minute pit stop at a burger joint where we sat down and ate. I wondered about his sense of planning, but, since he'd invited me out, I didn't presume to know more than he did. Once we finally got to the event, security literally closed the doors in our faces since there was a cut off time for admission. We'd gotten there just after the cutoff and now we were left out in the cold. The red flags were right; he didn't properly prepare for this date and had basically invited me to go on a wild goose chase with him. Although we could sustain fulfilling conversation, I thought his lack of planning rude. After that, I just was not that into him. We talked on the phone a couple more times, but I knew his lack of vision was a problem. What was really confusing to me was the fact that he was everything that I thought I wanted. I mistakenly thought that if I met someone with whom there was a high degree of compatibility on paper, there was no way we could fail in

---

[3]See David Richo's *How To Be An Adult in Relationships: The Five Keys to Mindful Loving*, (Boston, Massachusetts, 2002).

person! Since this guy was "qualified" to date me and I could put a check by most entries on the "date checklist" in my head, I thought he was the one!

A final LoveMeLesson I learned as a result of this experience taught me how compatibility is expressed through interaction, not by an admiration for looks, accomplishments or other superficial traits. Any titles or degrees one possesses do not necessarily reflect how a person will treat you. Ultimately, love amounts to a couple's ability to interact based on shared values, love, and respect. You become competent in loving others by loving yourself first. When you love yourself, you also set a standard that others must meet.

Single Moms are for Grown Ups

A single mom is already a spiritual subject, in other words, a grown up.

By virtue of the fact that she manages care for herself and that of her child(ren), she doesn't have the same time on her hands as women who don't have children. She doesn't have time for mates who cannot generally plan in advance, mates who have no vision for their lives, immature mates who are not emotionally intelligent or who don't possess sufficient social skills.

Dating a single mom is not for the faint of heart. It is a challenge for which not everyone is prepared. Dating a single mom is a challenge only for those who are up to it.

A single mom must date those who are similarly yoked, those who have developed some sense of discipline for themselves and who can recognize her skills as the strengths that they truly are. A single mom with a clear self-image can attract a mate with whom she can form a power couple since her strengths are now mirrored back to her.

Chapter Eight

@SingleMomM.O.G.U.Ls

@SingleMomM.O.G.U.Ls are mystics who know how to face challenges and overcome them. In other words, like a billionaire, a Single Mom M.O.G.U.L. handles her business. She doesn't just handle problems on a surface level. She is a first rate problem solver. Even further, she effectively uses proven processes to produce amazing results.

A Single Mom M.O.G.U.L. actively engages in her spiritual work. Undoubtedly, she has read many books, attended classes and workshops, participated in support groups, and watched plenty of the Oprah Winfrey Network's (OWN) Super Soul Sunday. She has even sought the professional help she needs.

She identifies her childhood issues and works to heal them. She doesn't look to her mate for any dimension of love she missed in childhood. A Single Mom M.O.G.U.L. has broken generational curses that threatened to enslave her and her children. Conversely, she doesn't live through her children or make the mistake of trying to provide them with things she feels like she didn't have. She defies any cultural limitations imposed upon her, relegating her to being "barefoot and pregnant" or carrying societal burdens like "a mule of the world."

She has learned to love herself, extends that love to her children and can even constructively express her love for her fellow (wo)man.

Finally, @SingleMomM.O.G.U.L.s aim high, set their goals and organize themselves to achieve them.

Truthfully, any single mom who knows her purpose, follows her dreams, and achieves her goals can be referred to as a Single Mom M.O.G.U.L. Just like business moguls are considered masters of industry, a Single Mom M.O.G.U.L. masters her own dynamic soul. She recognizes her incredible power within and sets about cultivating, managing and expressing it. A @SingleMomM.O.G.U.L.s is what we call a single mom who operates in the following realms:

M - Motherhood/Mastery/Magic/Miracles
O - Ownership
G - Growth and Development
U - Uncommon(ness)
L - Legacy

Motherhood/Mastery/Magic/Miracles - A mastery as well as a mystery, motherhood is a sublime leadership dimension. Motherhood denotes incredible strength, unconditional love, and a source of wisdom from which all life proceeds. @SingleMomM.O.G.U.Ls understand "Paradise lies at the foot of the Mother"; her holy status as "mother" represents a source of stability, confidence and abundance.

Single mom masters believe in their own knowledge and skills; she isn't so amateurish as to ask for everyone's advice before she can make decisions. Even though she needs help and support, a Single Mom M.O.G.U.L. maintains boundaries with others by not being too open to their opinions. Since she truly values her own experiences, both "positive" and "negative," she primarily draws upon them as references as opposed to what others think. Also, she does not overthink her decisions. She is not fearful of making bad life decisions since she deeply believes in herself.

Ownership - Although "it takes two to tango," a Single Mom M.O.G.U.L. takes 100% responsibility for her situation. Her mindset takes a cue from The Serenity Prayer in accepting that which she cannot change, her courage to change what she can, as well as practicing wisdom in knowing the difference. Therefore, a Single Mom M.O.G.U.L. does not see herself as a victim since she doesn't dwell on her mistakes. In her mind, mistakes are an opportunity to display her leadership skills, flexibility, and courage in meeting challenges head on.

@SingleMomM.O.G.U.Ls understand the importance of exercising emotional intelligence when interacting with others. Two aspects of emotional intelligence a Single Mom M.O.G.U.L. especially uses are empathy and "other-orientedness." Knowing that others are usually egocentric or primarily focused on their own interests, @SingleMomM.O.G.U.Ls know how to empathize with those whom they interact when they communicate, actively listening, asking follow-up questions, and tailoring her message to her audience.

Even further, @SingleMomM.O.G.U.Ls know better than to "judge a book by its cover" or take people at face value. Quickly, @SingleMomM.O.G.U.Ls assess the type of person with whom they're dealing whether based on a combination of psychological, personality, behavioral, or other communicative characteristics and interacts with them based on her understanding of them. In other words, a Single Mom M.O.G.U.L. can "read" those with whom she comes into contact and carefully manages her every interaction rather than be subject to it. In doing so, she does not relinquish her precious power nor does she give a false impression that she is needy or dependent.

Growth and Development - Spirituality is a priority for a Single Mom M.O.G.U.L. She knows her spiritual practices as a source from which all her blessings proceed. Her unshakeable faith is a basis upon which she acts without desperation, investing in herself and her future. She engages in regular self-care, delays gratification to further her education, and holds herself accountable to those who depend on her. She maintains a wholesome discipline in all areas of her life, including her financial, physical, and psychological well-being.

Uncommon(ness) - A Single Mom M.O.G.U.L. knows and accepts her journey as an uncommon one, incomparable to others. As such, she does not enter into practices that are not in her best interests, such as "keeping up with the Joneses" or "looking for love in all the wrong places," i.e., outside of herself. Conversely, she does not mistake her uncommon(ness) as a reason not to seek the help she needs or accept the support she deserves. She actively receives love and support from those who value her strengths and recognize her beauty.

Legacy - In all her communications, a Single Mom M.O.G.U.L. acts with an end in mind. She is not desperate. As a leader, she maintains her boundaries, sets an example, honors her agreements, and inspires confidence in others. A Single Mom M.O.G.U.L. has her priorities straight so there is no question about her motives, intentions, or messages.

She is an inspiring model of a spiritual woman who overcomes adversity to accomplish her goals and serve the world in the highest ways.

@SingleMomM.O.G.U.L.s Mindset Makeover - Assess, Conceive/Dream, & Express

When a single mom achieves a M.O.G.U.L mindset, she can attract anything she wants, including a billionaire.

In order to do so, a single mom may have to first transform her mindset through a "makeover." Unlike those we usually see on plastic surgery shows or as segments on a talk show, a @SingleMomM.O.G.U.L.s Mindset Makeover does not happen on the surface; it is a process that transforms her thinking, thereby transforming her in unseen ways before it is reflected on the outside. She develops new beliefs about herself. Once she believes she can have what she wants, she will see it.

One thing a single mom deals with in trying to make over her mindset is a lack of positive images to which she can refer. Often, we end up trying to force ourselves into an image that doesn't enhance or illuminate our best features. She can easily get discouraged or distracted by trying to fit into these molds.

However, this would be a mistake.

Instead of limiting ourselves to preconceived or unconscious images, a Single Mom M.O.G.U.L. must achieve a new vision of herself. She does this through the following steps:

1. Single Mom Selfie Image Evaluation- Since you attract who you are, use your past and current relationships to determine how you see yourself.

Our former and current relationships provide excellent mirrors, reflecting the ways we see ourselves. As the sayings go, "birds of a feather flock together" or "your network is your net worth." Everything we like or dislike in others reflects back to what we like or dislike in ourselves. If we find that we are miscommunicating, and being intentionally or unintentionally misread, we must make the necessary mindset adjustments to correct these issues. These changes will ultimately effect who we attract into our lives.

Some of these changes include:

- ridding yourself of negative people and thoughts as soon as possible,
- surrounding yourself with friends and support groups that reflect your best qualities, goals, and aspirations,
- improving our communication skills through assertiveness in asking for what we   want and refusing what we do not want, and
- improving self-care habits.

2. Visualization

A. Write a new makeover story reflecting your new ideal self, including your own Billionaire Boo. This new story should reflect the changes you determined that you want to make from your Single Mom Selfie Image Evaluation worksheet.

B. Create a vision board. Gather a poster board, old magazines, scissors, and glue sticks. Cut and glue images that represent your vision for your life. These images may be literal or metaphors. Include pictures of mates who reflect your Billionaire Boo, your ideal mate. Also, do not be afraid to dream big, include high end visions and locations. Be sure to include pictures of all your heart's desires, no matter the expense. Single moms often play themselves small due to our concerns for our children's well-being; however, being overly cautious with regard to our dreams can be a bad side effect.

In the words of Michelangelo, "The greater danger for most of us lies not in setting our aim too high and falling short; but in setting our aim too low and achieving our mark."

C. Set goals with deadlines. Use index cards (I prefer the big 5x8 ones) to set goals with deadlines. As an academic, my time is usually organized around semesters, half yearly increments without summers. When I set my goals, however, I find setting my goals on a quarterly basis works best for me. I review my goals at least twice daily, keeping my cards in my bag and taking them out when I have free moments.

3. Effective Expression: Become a "Meta Mama"

@SingleMomM.O.G.U.Ls effectively express themselves through "metacommunication" or communicating with wisdom. In other words, @SingleMomM.O.G.U.Ls engage in less talk and take more direct actions towards our goals since we understand "actions speak louder than words."

@SingleMomM.O.G.U.Ls "show, don't tell" their feelings of high self-worth. We do so by engaging in:

a. (A lot of) Self-care - Like moguls in other sectors, @SingleMomM.O.G.U.L.s minds her own business. Her business is a huge enterprise, but she's up to the challenge! @SingleMomM.O.G.U.Ls create a self-care regimen that will produce the results she wants to see reflected in a mirror. If she wants to see a six pack of rock hard abs, she finds or creates a regimen ensuring her core becomes strong and chiseled. If she wants to project an new image of confidence, she reprograms her self-image using affirmations, positive self-talk, and guided meditations. A Single Mom M.O.G.U.L. engages only in activities communicating high self-esteem.

b. "Show, Don't Tell" - When you determine your image and goals, change your vibration with yourself and others; open yourself by "Show, Don't Tell." To "Show, Don't Tell" is to meta-communicate about who you are and your understanding of your worth.

Another way to think of "Show, Don't Tell" is as an exercise in accepting yourself fully. Now that you have assessed your communication and decided on your standard (through LoveMeLessons), it is time to present yourself with confidence and presence.

"Show, Don't Tell" has several benefits. Not only does it magnetize our desires to us, it helps retrain our brains in regards to who we are. If low self-esteem has been a block in our success, acting "Show, Don't Tell" retrains our actions, renewing our minds. We reinforce our mind-body connection from which all of our actions proceed. However, when we "Show, Don't Tell" we show what we think of ourselves and tell afterwards. To do so is a new way of being for some of us who might even overthink before acting which becomes a stumbling block to our success. Thinking too much can lead to procrastination or reinforce a fear of success. Also, when we act first, we break the habit of talking too much, another common mental block.

Unfortunately, it is a common misconception that we only learn by thinking first. Most of our classroom models are based on sitting behind desks, listening to a teacher lecture, and regurgitating information. However, the truth is that we can learn by doing first. As such, we actually ingrain the lesson in our bodies versus our minds. We don't have to rely on our minds so heavily since our body has a memory of its own. I find that it's actually a relief not have to tax my mind and/or memory too heavily. I love it when my body executes good habits on its own without having to think or worry about it.

As a communications professor, I often encourage my students to "Show, Don't Tell" when delivering their assigned speeches. Although speaker anxiety is a very common condition, public speaking students are expected to manage their fears very early in the semester (the first week, even) to deliver an introduction speech to their classmates. One way I suggest that they manage their apprehension is to "fake it (confidence) until they make it." I support this suggestion with an anecdote about my early experiences as an instructor when I had to pretend I was my daughter when delivering lectures. My daughter, who is now in her final year of acting school, was born an actress and always gave her all to the songs she loved to sing and the animated stories she told. Whenever she "performed" you could see the veins in her neck pop out as she worked hard to hit her notes. When I first started teaching, I, like my daughter, would throw myself into delivering my lessons as a way of not being inhibited by my fearful thoughts. In this respect, I acted as if I was my gifted daughter until I acquired more experience. Just as it did for my daughter who was offered more than 10 scholarships to various drama programs and schools, dedication paid off, and I now enjoy much better teaching evaluations and reviews.

   c. Social media (as a) Solution-
       @SingleMomM.O.G.U.Ls use social media with
       care. Although social media can be a "feel good"
       outlet or distraction from overwhelming feelings, a
       Single Mom M.O.G.U.L. knows that her image can
       suffer due to oversharing, including posting too
       many pictures of her children, which can be unsafe.
       Also, posting too much unfiltered information or
       too many "social" pictures (e.g., partying, drinking,
       etc.) can cause undue judgement, stressing us out
       even more. @SingleMomM.O.G.U.Ls use various
       social media platforms to give and receive wisdom,
       support, and productive tips on managing our busy
       lives. @SingleMomM.O.G.U.Ls do not use social
       media to elicit sympathy, seek attention, or voice
       negative thoughts or emotions.

4. Choose a mate using a "Billion Dollar Standard"

Once a Single Moms realizes herself as a Single Mom M.O.G.U.L., she has many qualities in common with the world's most successful individuals, especially with regard to mastery when it comes to:

Faith
Excellence
Resourcefulness
Stick to it-ness
Vision
Networking/community building
Leadership
Abundant
Attractive
Follow through
Meditative
Balanced
Humorous (an ability to keep things in perspective and laugh at herself)
Flexibility
High standards
Wisdom
Courage
Strength
Creativity
Teacher
Loving
Caring

Having truthfully assessed her image, clarified her vision, and expressed her self-worth through her actions, @SingleMomM.O.G.U.L.s can attract Billionaire Boos. @Single MomM.O.G.U.L.s challenge themselves to date differently, making sure their dates accurately reflect their improved self-images. When she finally meets him, she does not compromise her standards (or hard work, for that matter), making sure that he passes David Richo's "head,

head, and gut"[4] test. Most importantly,
@SingleMomM.O.G.U.L.s maintain confidence, self-care,
and positive actions toward achieving their goals.

---

[4] Ibid.

Chapter Nine

A Billion Dollar Love Standard

What do the R&B singers Ciara and Monica have in common with Kimora Lee Simmons?

What is the common ground shared by Oprah Winfrey's collaborations with Toni Morrison, Iyanla Vanzant, Kim Whitley, Miss Robbie (of Sweetie Pies), and Evelyn Lozada? They represent rare, abundant business partnerships with @**SingleMomM.O.G.U.Ls**.

Contrary to what we might think, attracting a quality partner is a spiritual exercise, not one that takes place on the surface. In other words, attracting a high quality mate is not a matter of changing the length of one's hair or the size of one's behind or breasts. Attracting a Billionaire Boo is an outgrowth of our self-love by which our "love lights" shine.

Meeting my Billionaire Boo

When I experienced an initial attraction to my Billionaire Boo, I wasn't sure what was going on due to many changes I was going through at the time. He didn't look like my type, yet he stayed on my mind. Our first conversation happened at his retail store where he sold copies of the two books he'd written so far. As I flipped through them, I realized we shared a love of writing. I left the store with copies of both of his books; I read them from beginning to end as soon as I got home. I admired the structure of his writing, and I sent him a text to tell him so. We communicated back and forth in a friendly way, but our attraction was undeniable. We went out to eat and to movies, all while making each other laugh as we discovered shared values. He and I grew up in the same era; we married, had children and divorced at about the same time. I was most surprised to learn how much we had in common emotionally. For the first time in a long time, my relationship mirrored the way I interacted with the world. We shared similar temperaments, world views, and standards. We both respected the other's accomplishments. Our career paths were similar but not too much alike. In other words, we complimented each other's strengths while buttressing each other's weaknesses. Most importantly, my Billionaire Boo and I share an abundant mindset based on faith and self-love. (Did I mention that the subtitle of one his books is: "Living the Abundant Life?")

My Billionaire Boo sees my beauty, understands my humor, and values my intellect. Can I tell you how amazing it feels to give and take "attention, acceptance, affection, appreciation, and allowing?"[5]

Talk about Sweet Love!

When I look into the mirror of my new relationship, I am finally pleased with what I see! Through my LoveMeLessons, I learned self-love and attracted a Billionaire Boo who loves himself too. My new relationship reflects my sense of excellence, a wholesome discipline, flexibility, and an ability to grow.

---

[5] Ibid.

As we got to know each other, I did not make the mistake of changing my focus from my own self-care to tending to him. I was sure to keep my writing, goal setting, exercise, and creative production schedules. I stayed true to my LoveMeLessons by using my relationship as a platform to become a better me. As an added bonus, similarities in our professional backgrounds provide collaboration opportunities of which I've long dreamed.

Most importantly, my boo met my Billion Dollar standard; I *listened for love*, seeking first to understand, then be understood. As of this writing, we are fast approaching three-years of partnership, and our relationship is stronger than ever!

Because my Billionaire Boo shares my spiritual values for abundance, our new life together includes our mutual visions of beautiful homes, luxury cars, a maid—the best of everything.

I would not have achieved my LoveLife goals had I not maintained my Billion-Dollar Standard.

Even before I met my Billionaire Boo, even when I was still growing through trial and error, I never got down on myself. What's more, I never got into a dating habit of complaining about my ex or anyone else with whom I was involved because I understood their existence in my life reflected my self-image. Based on my SingleMomM.O.G.U.L. mindset, talking negatively about my mate or men, in general, made *me* look bad since it was really myself about whom I talked negatively. With regard to my own negative traits, I either accepted them or eliminated them. Again, I take responsibility for any traits I saw in my (past or present) mate since it reflects my choice to enter a relationship with them. Certainly, I am not a "damsel in distress" needing to be rescued nor a girl child who cannot be held responsible for her actions. As an adult, I am clear about what constitutes "deal breaking" behavior versus differences I can work out. I can fight my own battles. I understand the difference between right and wrong, and I don't need others' input in making life decisions. It shocked me to learn how many women, young and old, engage in hours and hours of destructive talk, complaining about men in their lives as if their words, as well as their men, do not reflect their self-images. Can they not hear themselves? When in the company of women who begin such a conversation, I quickly shut them down. I explain I am just not that interested in joining any pity parties or, at my age, debating our love lives. In other words, "girl talk" is for young people whom I do not idolize nor want to switch places. I'm clear about my identity as a Single Mom M.O.G.U.L., and talking about problems over and over again does not solve them. As a Single Mom M.O.G.U.L., I only focus on solutions and results. For @SingleMomM.O.G.U.Ls, a Billionaire-Dollar-Love Standard ensures we enter into love relationships valuing our true worth.

On Becoming More

"In order to have more, you have to become more." Jim Rohn

Before I attracted my love, I achieved my personal and professional goals including finishing my Ph.D. and earning tenure. During this time, my children also finished high school and left home for college. All of these achievements required more from me than I even thought possible. Not only did I have to pass my examinations, write my dissertation, orally defend my work, regularly engage in scholarly activity, lead committees, attend meetings, advocate for positions I believed in, and watch out for exploiting and backstabbing colleagues, I had to do the homework that prepared me for these professional tests.

I wouldn't say it was easy to simultaneously finish the Ph.D., raise my children alone, and earn tenure, but with prayer, patience, and perseverance, I achieved these goals. Sometimes when people ask me how I did it, I am tempted to tell them it was a #SingleMomMiracle, or an accomplishment that single moms, like me, regularly make happen but for which we rarely get credit. Single moms go to school and work, raise their children, manage their households, accomplish their personal and professional goals every day, but very little fanfare is made of it. On the contrary, single moms are often stereotyped as poor and uneducated as well as maligned and scapegoated for societal ills. Even worse, single moms are blamed for raising their children alone with no mention of absent fathers. In other words, single moms are often (mis)represented by who they are not instead of who they are.

#SingleMomMiracles not only reflect all that single moms make happen but a single mom herself.

A single mom who knows herself, has a clear vision, and expresses herself effectively can attract everything she wants! She can manifest #SingleMomMiracles.

It was not until I achieved clarity of vision that my goals manifested. There were specific practices that I engaged in to get out of my rut, and before I knew it, I had what I wanted! The difference between the times I was faltering and my moments of success boiled down to a few key practices.

When I left graduate school to accept a job before completing my dissertation, I practiced what Deepak Chopra refers to in *The Seven Spiritual Laws of Success* as "detachment." In using "The Law of Detachment," I engaged in a spiritual practice through which I maintained a balance of identifying a clear goal, yet not becoming too tied to a certain outcome, in this case, a Ph.D. In fact, I could see all seven of Chopra's Laws at work in my life. After many years of study, I used spiritual practices to achieve what I wanted versus trying too hard, or engaging in "hard work" or a of lot effort, thus reflecting "The Law of Least Effort."

Before I attracted my Billion-Dollar Love, I became more. I got beyond a threshold within myself. Even though by some standards, as an effect of "The Law of Pure Potentiality," I'd accomplished a lot by that point, there were still some important milestones that I hadn't accomplished, and I wasn't satisfied. I doubled down and focused on achieving these goals. I prioritized these goals as non-negotiable and set about realizing them even though I had to work hard to develop new skills. In other words, despite the challenges of being a single mom, I achieved a mastery in my life's work which is also (thankfully) the field in which I work. Since my job is closely tied to my life's purpose ("The Law of Dharma"), I was able to serve ("The Law of Giving") the university as well as the community in which I work through it. I pushed beyond inner distractions of scarcity, fear of success, procrastination, and perfectionism as well as outer distractions, such as, societies' definitions and narratives projecting disparaging images of single moms, like me. I ignored those who didn't believe in me and separated myself from those who didn't treat me well, careful not to create harmful effects for myself through "The Law of Karma." It was "The Law of Intention and Desire" that ultimately pushed me beyond my threshold and into an abundant realm in which I could attract my heart's deepest desires easily and effortlessly.

Achieving Clarity of Vision/ A Final Push

One thing I wanted to achieve but had not yet happened between the time I earned tenure and met my Billionaire Boo was to publish in an academic journal. Publishing scholarly articles is one of the most important exercises an academic can perform. I had submitted several articles to scholarly journals in my field, but had yet to have one accepted. I worked hard and long (for over a year!) on an article that I considered my best effort yet. I submitted an article to a top journal, but instead of it being accepted, it was assigned a "revise and resubmit" status which meant I had more work to do. On top of that, the revisions that were suggested by reviewers were extensive. Although the article was not outright rejected, the number of changes that needed to be made was enough to discourage anyone.

I'll admit, I WAS discouraged. I was disappointed that my ideas weren't met with more enthusiasm. However, I knew the reviewers' comments were valuable, and I knew that the only way to achieve my goal was to heed the reviewers' advice. So, despite the amount of work the revisions entailed, I set about making the changes. I engaged in habits that I'd never used before. I created a routine of prayer, reading, writing, and rest. I wrote my writing goals down and reviewed them frequently, and for the first time ever, I read books about academic writing.

For the past several years, I'd met with a colleague, Elizabeth, every week to check in on our writing goals. While I was working on my article, she was writing her dissertation, finishing her Ph.D. in Art History. At about the time I received my revision letter, another professor I knew started an academic writing support group on a social media site. I joined the group even though I felt inferior to the other members. I put my ego aside and participated as fully as possible, despite my insecurities. Also, I didn't put a limit on how much work I was willing to put in. Even though I was already in one support group, I joined this new one. Soon, I was getting beyond my issues and actually learning how to best implement the suggested improvements. My job was keeping me busier than ever, but I still managed to make my writing a priority, sticking with it and checking in with my support groups regularly. I found myself moving out of isolation and perfectionism into new habits, helping me make progress with my revisions.

I was also inspired around this time to create a vision board. Although I'd grown up seeing my father use them, I never took the time to actually create one for myself. Honestly, I saw it more as a creative endeavor than one of goal setting. Boy, did I miss the mark on that one! In less than 90 days I attracted goals that I had only had fleeting thoughts about but included. Through my vision boards, I learned the necessity of vividly imagining and even *feeling* our desires in order to manifest them.

I didn't really perceive it initially, but through my new visionary practices, I became more than myself. I taught myself to write better, both content wise and technically. I'd pushed myself beyond limits that were still dogging me even though I felt I'd put in so much work already. I did not give in to my exhaustion or feelings of being overwhelmed by the complex subject matter about which I was writing. Nor did I allow all the things wrong with my writing to stop me from focusing on what was right with it. I'd persevered and found my way to my process, representing my growth and development as an eternal Truth.

It took me longer than I liked, especially since I had to deal with, not one but two car accidents in which my cars were totaled and I suffered minor neck and back injuries. However, I did finish my revisions and resubmitted my article. I had finally broken through to a higher plane, a spiritual Self whose results exceeded those previously thought possible.

A "Billionaire Boo" Blueprint

With a mindset of self-love and gratitude, I focused on my biggest goals while still maintaining a dating blueprint I'd developed for myself over the years.

I now refer to this formula as my "Billionaire Boo" Blueprint.

My Billionaire Boo Blueprint is a five-step process @Single Mom M.O.G.U.Ls can use when they meet potential mates. The steps consist of the following:

1. **Evaluate** - Upon meeting a potential mate, a Single Mom M.O.G.U.L. introduces herself to her new prospect while evaluating them to determine how they mirror her. She wonders to herself: Does her potential mate reflect her best qualities back on herself, especially with regard to self-care, resource management, goal setting and achievement, personal

development, setting priorities, etc.? If the answers are "yes," she might proceed to get to know them.

2. **Relate** - With no pressure involved, a Single Mom M.O.G.U.L. can begin to listen (not over talk) to a potential mate to see the degree to which they have something in common. This is the stage in which a Single Mom M.O.G.U.L. "listens for love," actively probing and prompting to find out the habits of her prospect. She also establishes her standards for a mate, mostly through her actions. She reinforces her self-care and establishes her priorities by demonstrating them, not talking about them. She especially does not make the mistake of falling into a "service trap," of over-helping another to the neglect of one's own interests.

3. **Negotiate** - No relationship exists without conflict. Since it is necessary in getting to know another, a Single Mom M.O.G.U.L. approaches this stage with her standards in mind but appropriately uses flexibility in communication. Most importantly, she uses this stage to see how her potential mate handles conflict. Do they tell the truth or lie? Do they process their anger appropriately or strike out in blind rage? Will they take responsibility in the situation, or do they blame everything on her? Since a Single Mom M.O.G.U.L. is assertive in tackling problems, she uses her best communication skills and practices while managing their interaction. She heeds any red flags and practices detachment in resolving any issues, even if it means detaching herself from the relationship.

4. **Date** - Once a Single Mom M.O.G.U.L. is clear that her prospect is worthy of dating, she can now enter into a period of dating in which she can seriously communicate with him. She can open up to him, continuing to check for safety in doing so. Since she is still busy taking care of herself and accomplishing her goals, this stage entails the establishment of a routine

between them in which she doesn't change her priorities but can easily work in her date.

5. **Mate** - Having successfully passed through the first four stages of the Billionaire Boo Standard, a Single Mom M.O.G.U.L. can now enter into a serious commitment. As two mature individuals, a Single Mom M.O.G.U.L. and her Billionaire Boo decide how they will practice their monogamous relationship in a way that works best for them. Their relationship is a responsible one in which they successfully manage their responsibilities individually and together. Both are both happy and satisfied with the give and take of their love since it represents the best they both have to offer.

Chapter Ten

No Easy Wins

"Tell No Lies. Claim No Easy Victories." Amilcar Cabral,
Revolution in Guinea (1969)

Take a moment to imagine the following scenario:

You are a woman between 35 -65 whose children are all
grown and may even have children of their own. One or
more of your grown children overly depends on you
financially.

You are working a job that you don't love for two reasons:
1. You have never pursued your dreams in a disciplined,
sustained way; 2. You didn't adequately prepare for your
future when you were younger.

You have a small group of women friends with whom you
talk regularly. You all laugh often, but it is with no real joy
since your conversations are usually at the expense of
others.

You don't have and may have never experienced a healthy
love relationship. Since you were a teenager, you seem to
attract the same type of men and relationships over and
over again to disastrous results. You usually rush into
relationships without knowing your prospective mate well,
only to regret it. Now, you've been alone for an extended
period of time even though you and your friends often talk
about men, dating, and relationships.

Not only are you not prepared for retirement, you don't have anyone with which to share the experience or expenses.

Does this scenario sound like someone you know? Or worse, do you seem to be headed in this direction yourself?

Common Mistakes to Avoid

Becoming a Single Mom M.O.G.U.L. is a complex yet achievable objective, but it is important to avoid certain mistakes along the way.

Unfortunately, single moms often compromise our standards by seeking "easy wins" or immediate solutions to the alienation, exhaustion, and misrepresentation we regularly experience. We may use codependent habits we developed in childhood into our adult experience as a single mom leading to disastrous results.

When we rush into solutions, we are not seeking our excellence. We are settling for an immediate option not in keeping with our Billionaire Standard. When we make mistakes, we set ourselves back, delaying our Billionaire Boos' entrances into our lives.

The following are some common mistakes Single Moms make:

- Rushing into a relationship seeking fulfillment before establishing stable foundation for self,
- Escaping through various means such as partying, drinking/drugs, sleeping, or sex,
- Focusing on outside appearance instead of inside spiritual development,

- Settling/aiming for expectations that are too low
- Setting expectations that are too high, reflecting inflexible communication, as well as an unclear self-image,
- Letting family, friends, or grown children get in the way of your relationship, and
- Going back to old relationships.

When overwhelmed, we are easily distracted. We can focus on what we think we are missing instead of focusing on what we have, thus, increasing our fears, making us more desperate. Instead of using our time as a single mom to cultivate ourselves as @SingleMomM.O.G.U.Ls, we can get stuck in patterns that stunt our growth and delay our dreams. We can put our self-care needs last, mistakenly justifying desperate acts as "doing what I have to do for my kids." We seek validation from others, attempting to ward off feelings of loneliness, isolation, and failure.

We try to avoid an emptiness inside by seeking out a relationship before we are in our right minds. As such, we choose a mate out of an unhealthy place rather than a place of strength. By refusing to be alone first, we refuse to do our necessary preparation work, indicating that we are (at the least) lazy and/or entitled.

Another way we misdirect our focus is by trying to communicate our value through our clothes, hair, and looks. We become preoccupied with looking like a Single Mom M.O.G.U.L. instead of acting like one. We try to attract a Billionaire Boo with our looks instead of through our spiritual practices. We mistakenly buy into a false logic that how we look determines who we will date. We focus on looks as a quick fix to the complexity of our dating lives as single moms. Consequently, we make the same mistakes over and over again, attracting mates who treat us like shiny objects (trophies). Instead of practicing self-care and other "laws of success," we are unmindful of the ways we try too hard.

Conversely, without a clear image of self, a single mom may make the mistake of entering into a relationship based on looks or other superficial qualities, or worse, try to make it work with whoever comes along. When a single mom has no clear standards set for herself or her mate, she can make a difficult situation worse for herself as well as her children.

In seeking to "fake it" or imitate a Single Mom M.O.G.U.L., a single mom may set unrealistic goals about a potential mate, especially with regard to their financial status or their looks. Having too easily bought into a cultural myth of "tall, dark, and handsome" or a "Rich Prince" who comes in to "sweep her off her feet" (read: deliver her from her responsibilities), a single mom may look for a rich mate rather than listening for a lasting love. Unfortunately, a single mom with expectations that are too high comes to find out that she has disillusioned herself with someone who can look like a Billionaire Boo but doesn't act like one. Ultimately, those who we look to "to save us" are usually the same people we need to be "saved from" in the end.

A single mom who overly relies on the opinions of others dooms her relationships to failure before they begin. Even if well meaning, our families', friends', and children's opinions can echo or even amplify our insecurities, doubts, and fears. Overly relying on others' opinions about our love lives only serves to limit our movement toward Mastery.

Often, single moms respond to their nontraditional relationship status by going back to an old relationship. Although this situation may feel comfortable, it is often a "situation-ship," reflecting an unhealthy pattern of "fixing" long term problems with temporary solutions. When single moms return to old relationships, it is often because we have no Big Picture plan in mind. Consequently, failure to plan ensures our plan to fail.

Chapter Eleven

A "SingleMom Selfie" Image Examination

Since all of our answers lie within ourselves, we must do an honest self-check to assess where we are and where we are not.

A good tool to use in determining our positioning is "A Single Mom Selfie" image examination. In this exercise, we can use our close personal relationships as self-reflections when we cannot get a clear view of ourselves otherwise. It's kind of like taking a selfie and posting it only to realize that it projects more than you meant to reveal like your bedroom is a mess or you have staged a scene instead of taken an "in the moment" photo. Through this exercise, we can use our immediate surroundings and circle to get a clearer perspective on the images we project to the world.

For this exercise, we list five people with whom we interact regularly and reflect on the ways they accurately reflect our self-image or ways that they distort our self-image. We can also use our surrounding environments to gauge how effective we are in attracting who and what we want in our lives. When we take an honest inventory of ourselves, we can determine if we are hitting our mark or where we need to make adjustments.

1. List the top five people with which you interact regularly.

    1. _____
    2. _____
    3. _____
    4. _____
    5. _____

2. List the qualities about them that reflect back to qualities you love or hate about yourself.

    Qualities I love:

    Qualities I hate:

3. What can you do to enhance the qualities you dislike in yourself?

4. What can you do to minimize the qualities you dislike in yourself?

5. Is there a difference between how you see yourself and how the world sees you?

6. What measures can you take project an image of yourself that better communicates how you see yourself? (Remember: "show, don't tell")

About the Author

Maisha S. Akbar, Ph.D. is a scholar, producer, director, activist and playwright who produces creative and business platforms countering gender, race and class based oppression.

After completing her Master of Arts degree in Folklore from the University of California at Berkeley, Maisha went on to pursue her doctorate in Communications Studies (Performance Studies) at the University of Texas at Austin where she won academic awards for her cultural production. Once she began her academic career in the University of Georgia system, she continued post graduate work at Northwestern University as well as professional development through an Association of Theatre in Higher Education Leadership program, among others. After earning tenure, Maisha developed the first theatre and performance studies academic program in her University's 120 year history, transforming the campus as well as the surrounding community by producing popular and cutting edged art productions.

Maisha is active in several academic and professional organizations. She facilitates her performance based workshops and presentations to such institutions as the Fifth Annual Faculty Women of Color in Academia conference, Alpha Kappa Alpha Sorority, Inc., Fort Valley State University College of Arts and Sciences and Mercer University Center for Southern Studies. In addition to a self- empowerment platform for single moms like herself, Dr. Akbar serves students, fellow educators of color, women and Historically Black College and University communities through her success trainings in "raising your standards." For more information contact her 229-395-4534.

Connect with Dr. Akbar on social media:

Website – www.billionaimesprefersinglemoms.com

Facebook - @SingleMomMoguls

Twitter - @SingleMomMoguls

Instagram - SingleMomMoguls

Transform your group, organization or community through the "How to Avoid the Service Trap" workshop

Participants are empowered to help them achieve individual and/or organizational goals through communications based solutions.

Your group will learn to avoid obstacles that keep them overworked, exhausted as well as socially and financially under-rewarded. Strategies for success through "raising the standard" are shared and rehearsed.

How to Avoid the Service Trap imparts wisdom as well as practical suggestions on creating a mindset and habits from which to achieve personal and professional success. Each workshop includes tools, exercises and training tailored to it's members. How to Avoid the Service Trap is ideal for the following groups:

> college and university faculty
> church groups
> professional organizations
> non profit organizations
> service organizations
> government employees and officials
> students and educators

Made in the USA
Columbia, SC
07 June 2019